재미동포 이성재 시인의 영시와 한국어 번역판

A collection of the poems published in English and Korean

# 홀로 아리랑
# Hollo Arirang

Not lonely, but only Arirang, Hollo Arirang

S.J. Peter Lee
이성재

(증정 사인용)

지은이

詩鄕 이 성 재

S.J. Peter Lee,Ph.D.

도장(印)

이詩

성鄕

재

# 홀로 아리랑

초판 1쇄 인쇄 | 2023년 12월 12일
지은이 | 이성재
펴낸이 | 이재욱(필명:이승훈)
펴낸곳 | 해드림출판사
주 소 | 서울 영등포구 경인로82길 3-4(문래동1가 39)
센터플러스빌딩 1004호(07371)
전 화 | 02-2612-5552
팩 스 | 02-2688-5568
E-mail | jlee5059@hanmail.net

등록번호 제2013-000076
등록일자 2008년 9월 29일

ISBN 979-11-5634-567-1

Anthology Dedicated
to My Beloved Family

나의 마음을 전하고 싶은
사랑하는 나의 가족에게

# TO MY BELOVED FAMILY

From afar in the Far East
I came to the land of opportunities
Without knowing shortcuts or easy ways

I made a long detour including a stopover in Germany
It was a long and tiring journey of life
With frustration and nostalgia taking turns
Often I wanted to go back to my home country

Never did I forget the future of my children
And the children of my children
During my long and tired days
Even today, we are all together

We, now include three sons and three daughters-in-law
Four grandsons and their cousins, four more grandsons
Together, we are a successful and blessed family
In the land of opportunities

My dear sons and grandsons
You all have bright futures ahead of you
I have done my job as well as I could
And you all made me to be proud

It's almost the time for my soul to see
My own Mom, Dad and siblings in the fatherland
I then will be returning to the Gate of Heaven
The home of my Eternal Life.

God bless you, I love you all.

## 사랑하는 나의 가족

멀고 먼 동방의 나라에서
쉽게 오는 지름길을 몰라
먼 길을 돌아왔노라 독일을 거쳐
기회의 땅 미국에

때로는 좌절과 향수에 젖은
고되고 긴 삶의 여정이었기에
고향으로 돌아가고 싶었지만

힘들고 오랜 세월에도
자손 대대의 장래를 잊지 않고
우리 함께 오늘 여기까지 왔노라.

3명 3명 그리고 4명 또 4명
아들과 며느리 그리고 손자 또 손자
성공하고 축복받은 가정
이 기회의 나라에서

내 사랑하는 아들과 손자들이여
너희들의 미래는 밝게 빛나니
나는 그저 나의 임무에 충실했으며
너희들은 우리를 자랑스럽게 했노라

이제 나의 영혼은 조국에 있는
부모형제를 만나러 갈 때가 되었네
그리고 이곳으로 다시 돌아올 것이다

사랑하는 나의 가족에게
더 많은 신의 축복이 내리기를

## Foreword

Hollo Arirang,

Solo in hollo, not lonely, but a recital of only Arirang, Hollo Arirang.

A touching solo in hollo followed by grandeur chorus and orchestra, Hollo Arirang

Poetry is a media transcends the cultural and social ideology to each other. The poems in the anthology were drafted and composed in English first then converted in Korean considering differences in languages and the meanings of poetry in socio-cultural differences in the West and East. It was not an easy task. That's the reason that the book is called an English-Korean anthology, not the other way around.

Expressions of poet primes the appreciations of readers and touches their hearts.

The pure sound is conveyed by the pure mind.

S.J. Peter Lee

## 책머리에

홀로 아리랑

홀로 불렀다. 그러나 나는 외롭지 않았다. 혼자 힘차게 노래한 홀로 아리랑, 가슴을 파고드는 솔로에 이어 웅장한 합창과 오케스트라가 울려 퍼졌다.

시는 서로의 문화적 사회적 관념을 초월하는 매체가 된다. 이 시집에 실린 시는 먼저 영어로 짓고 쓴 후 언어의 차이를 극복하고 시의 원래 의미를 살리기 위해 동서양의 사회적 문화적 차이점을 최대한 관찰하여 한국어로 번역하는 데는 상당한 어려움도 있었음을 말씀드린다. 그래서 이 시집을 한영이 아닌 영한 시집이라 하였다.

시인의 표현은 독자들의 감성을 유도하고 생각을 공유하는 것이다. 그 역할에 들어맞는 시로 인정받았으면 좋겠다.

아름다운 소리는 순수한 마음에 의해 전해질 것으로 믿는다.

詩鄕 이성재

## Review

Poet S.J. Peter Lee has given a great gift to humanity with the anthology, documenting in his poetry his thoughts and experiences about the human conditions in time and place.

In poetry such as poet Lee's, we can achieve peace and inter-cultural understanding. There are universal and cosmic meanings in this book. Poetry transcends national boundaries and limitations of language barriers, when it is written in multi languages.

Like the American Poet, Robert Frost, Peter Lee has stood at the crossroads to choose less traveled roads, the wanderer, the world traveler knows. He will let us follow as he expresses his moods and observations, going from Korea to Europe, America and more.

Peter wrote his poems in English and Korean. I have followed his writings(translations) in English only pointing out the areas where differences in cultural and social meanings appear. The vision, the philosophy, the emotion and the quality of this natural and gifted poet, are all his own. Peter Lee created a beautiful book in which we can find love, wonderment, joy and celebration of life.

Mary Rudge, Poet Laureate
2010 Nominee for
Nobel Peace Prize

## 서평

이성재 베드로 시인의 시집은 인간이 처한 시간과 공간에 따라 갖게 되는 생각과 경험을 시로써 기록한 것으로 인간 메리럿지에게 커다란 선물을 가져다주었다.

우리는 광대무변하고 다방면의 뜻과 내용을 담고 있는 이 시집에 실린 시를 통해 평화와 다문화 사회를 이해할 수 있을 것이다. 또한 여러 나라말로 번역된 시는 국경과 언어의 장벽을 넘을 수 있기 때문이다.

미국의 로버트 프로스트 시인처럼 이성재 시인도 방랑자나 세상을 돌아다니며 여행하는 사람들만이 알 수 있는 "남들이 많이 가지 않은 길"을 선택하려고 네거리 교차로에 서 있었다. 그는 한국에서 유럽의 여러 나라, 그리고 미국 등지에서 지내온 세월 동안 보고 느낀 것들을 시에 담아 전하면서 우리가 따라오기를 기다리고 있다.

나는 이성재 시인의 한영시 창작과 번역을 지켜보면서 문화적 사회적 이해의 차이로 인해 발생하는 단어의 선택이나 구절의 뜻과 표현에 관하여 상의할 수 있었다. 창작을 위한 비전이나 철학과 감성 그리고 시의 품위는 모두가 작가 자신의 것이다. 삶의 환희와 축제, 인간의 사랑과 경이로움을 독자들은 이 시집에서 찾을 수 있을 것이다.

메리 럿지, 계관시인
2010년 노벨 평화상 후보자

홀로아 리 랑

# Hollo Arirang

## *Table of Contents*

# Haiku Poetry

*Short Verses with 5-7-5 Letter Phrases*
*in Three Lines*

## An Ant

A tiny ant hanging still
at the edge of a pine needle
measuring it's body weight

개미 한 마리
솔잎 끝에 매달려
몸무게 달기

## Day Fly

Let's get together today
it's the request of a day fly
Can we meet tomorrow?

오늘 만나자
하루살이의 부탁
내일은 어때

Cheek turned away in red
before to say a word
the virgin rose in bud

말하기 전에
얼굴이 빨개지는
순진한 장미

Cried while walking
laughed in sadness
life of wooden spooners

걷다가 울다가
서러워서 웃었다
흙수저 인생

## *Pilgrimage*

Lightning in dark sky
on the pilgrimage to Jerusalem
saw the other side of heaven

## 순례길

번갯불 번쩍
예루살렘 순례길
천국의 저쪽

## *The Face of Mother*

In the hazy moonshine
a dream gone far with wind
the face of my mother

## 어머니 얼굴

흐린 달빛 속
바람에 날려간 꿈
어머니 얼굴

Ah nearby, yet distant
two nations across a narrow strait
love and hate of uneasy neighbors

가깝고도 먼
바다 건너 두 나라
불편한 이웃

The silver cross on a necklace
hitting the hearts of women and Amen
shouting John 3:16

은빛 십자가
목에 매달려 아멘
요한 3:16

At sunset after a long journey
smoking chimney of village homes
the nostalgia of vagabonds

해 질 무렵에
시골집 굴뚝 연기
나그네 설움

Sparkling in the shinny glasses
lift up for a toast for all
sound of colliding champagne glasses

이슬비 술잔
모두 높이 들었다
샴페인 축배

Born in the mountain ridge
lived here hundred and thousand years
the hometown of redwood trees

여기서 출생
조상대대 수백 년
소나무 고향

Confused with the seasons of years
forget-me-not flowers in the green house
when is the spring time?

계절을 잊고
온실에 핀 물망초
봄은 언제지

Gone and gone again thousand of years
yet, it's returning again and again
the last day of December

섣달 그믐날
수천 년이 지나도
다시 또 오네!

Seven years in silence
the larva in dark underground
chirring of cicadas

7년의 세월
암흑과 침묵 속에
매미의 울음

Alone in the autumn night
lost my way in maze and haze
the remaining life schedule

가을밤 홀로
미로에서 헤매다
인생 이정표

Lightning and thundering
the message of God
easy not to understand

번갯불 뇌성
하느님의 메시지
이해가 안 돼

## *The Relationship*

Me alone it can't be untied
even together couldn't be untangled
the relationship of you and me

혼자 못 풀고
함께 풀 수 없는 것
너와 나 사이

## *True Friend*

Another one like me
the more is the better
the true friends

또 하나의 나
많을수록 좋겠다
진정한 친구

Fell asleep
the light of longing on bright
the pain of love

당신 생각을
켜놓은 채 잠들다
사랑의 아픔

A kiss on the cheek
a heart breaking hug
and the good bye next

빰에다 키스
가슴 터지는 포옹
다음은 이별

## The Fallen Leaves

Memories of red and yellow
swept by the wind
sadness of fallen leaves

## 낙엽

바람에 날린
노랗고 빨간 추억
낙엽의 슬픔

## Only You

Good to see one
better to see one for long
it's you and me

보니 좋았다
오래 보니 더 좋다
바로 너와 나

Aim high
jumped with empty hands
advantage of the poor

높이 오르자
빈손으로 뛰었다
가난의 장점

Loved others to start with
forgave others at the end
a person with no sin

사랑도 했다
끝내 용서도 했다
죄 없는 사람

## *The Snail*

The first in the world
architect of mobile homes
is the carpenter snail

## 달팽이

이 세상 최초
모빌 홈 건축가는
달팽이 목수

## *The Eraser*

Wrong in many ways
erased and corrected one by one
myself crumbled in pieces

## 지우개

내 잘못한 것
하나 하나 고치다
가루가 된 몸

Your name is
as it's the priming water
pumps the blood in my heart

너의 이름은
내 심장 뛰게 하는
마중물 같아

In the cold battlefield
unfinished dream of returning to home
the wish of wounded soldier

차가운 전선
고향에 가지 못한
패잔병 소원

Thought it is gone and forgotten
coming back in dreams and haze
unforgotten and forgotten first love

잊을 만하면
꿈속에 나타나는
첫사랑 그대

The spring has come already
followed the next to winter
the season prepared in advance

겨울 뒤에는
봄이 이미 있었다
준비된 계절

Rainbow in Winter
too cold to be stretched
hunchback icicle

겨울 무지개
허리 굽은 고드름
추워 못 폈다

My heart beats sadly
80th anniversary of liberation
still the divided fatherland

가슴 아프다
해방된 지 80년
분단의 조국

## *The Heart of Green frog*

The summer rain front
pouring sadly as it's crying
the soul of green frog

여름 장맛비
짓궂게도 내리네
청개구리 넋

## *Paradise*

Lengthening shadows
Parallel to the road of pilgrimage
paradise at the end

## 천국

뻗친 그림자
순례길에 평행선
저 끝이 천국

Sound of church bell

the sinners and saints

pray together for love and peace

성당 종소리

죄인 성인 다 함께

사랑과 평화

Burned my own body

to shine your future

the candlelight revolution

내 몸을 태워

너의 앞을 밝혔다

아, 촛불혁명

Grabbed even a bit of straw
when fell into deep water
the principles of faith

물에 빠지면
지푸라기도 잡다
믿음의 원리

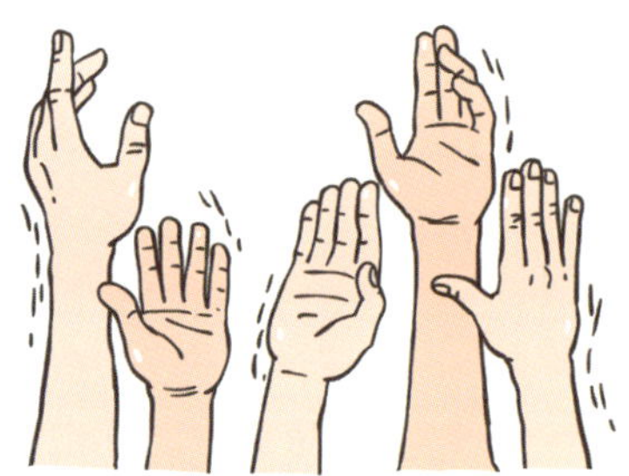

Sound of church bell
sound of wooden gong
in the hand of monk
it's the sound of eternity

교회 종소리
스님의 목탁 소리
구원의 소리

The sound of machine gun
from the sky, on the ground
The soul of 518

기관총 소리
하늘에서 땅에서
518 영혼

The past of politicians
usage alterations of human life
as the future of convicts

정치인 과거
인생의 용도변경
죄수의 미래

## The Lot

Born with a penny in the mouth
the life too heavy to carry
is the fate - not a chosen road

## 흙수저 운명

주어진 운명
삶의 무게 못이긴
흙수저 인생

## Fireflies

Burned its' own body
to brighten the dark night
the soul of fireflies

## 반딧불

내 몸을 태워
어둔 밤 불 밝히다
반딧불 영혼

Irrelevant promise
gone with wind
is the oath in vain

뜬금포 약속
바람에 날려버린
허무한 맹세

Friends, my dear friends
life is a vagabond
be not lonely, wander together

친구야 친구
삶은 나그네의 길
함께 가려나

Live in dirt and sweat
holding mom and dad's hands
nostalgia of vagabond

흙에 살리라
엄마 아빠 손 잡고
떠돌이 향수

The wrinkles of life
more beautiful than
the layers of floral leaves
a lovely couple in twilight

세월의 주름
꽃보다 아름다워
황혼의 부부

The sky and sea
kissed at the end of horizon
varnished the earth

하늘과 바다
수평선 맞닿은 곳
사라진 육지

The person I dearly miss
knowing she wouldn't return
though awaiting heart always

그리움이란
못 오는 줄 알면서
기다리는 것

Dreamed boyond dream
though the life is such an incompletion
it only leaves remorseful footprints

꿈을 피워도
아쉬움만 남기는
인생 미완성

Over the storm and waves
wanted to live round and smooth
as the shiny pebbles at beach

풍파를 넘어
둥글게 살아가리
조약돌처럼

Believing myself made me
be able to overcome difficulties in life
that was a blessing for success

나를 믿은 건
어려움을 이겨낸
성공의 축복

Sound of falling leave
crickets on the wave of autumn wind
echoed trembling chirpings

낙엽의 소리
풀벌레 울음소리
슬픈 콘서트

Song of a poet
it's the dream in the past
kept folded for a while

시인의 노래
잠시 접어 두었던
지난날의 꿈

Lapse of memory of the day
mushroom cloud over the land of Hiroshima
a transient light and shadow

빛과 그림자
히로시마 핵폭탄
망각의 그날

Flew by the wind
a spore of dandelion
to a far new land

바람을 타고
민들레 홀씨 되어
날아간 먼 곳

The time gone for
longing of mother's love
the winkles on every node
is the trace of love

모정의 세월
옹이 박힌 주름살
사랑의 흔적

Passion of a vagabond
comes and gone
like the soul of rainbow

뜨내기 연정
피었다 사라지는
무지개 영혼

Rodary in hand
counted the beads by heart
commandments for life

손에 든 묵주
가슴으로 굴리다
삶의 십계명

# Aphorism Poetry

*Free Style Haiku - A Transformation*

## Be Faithful Present

Ask not
the past of life
ask for the present
though today is in dying
tomorrow delivers a present again

## 오늘에 살다

과거를 묻지마세요
지금에 충실할지다
오늘은 이미 죽어가고 있지만
내일은 또 다른 오늘을 가져올지다

## The River of Sibling

The tears of mother
flowing down in the night
made the river of sibling

## 형제의 강

어머니 눈물
밤에만 흐르다
형제의 강 되다

## The Pumpkin Flower

The homely pumpkin flowers
no one looked at it
the shiny golden pumpkin
everyone loved it

## 호박꽃

못생긴 호박꽃
눈길도 받지 못했다
황금빛 익은 호박
사랑받았다

## First Love

Her happiness caused me jealous
her misery life made me sick
love again, it's a headache
First Love!
no news is a good news

## 첫사랑

행복하다니 배가 아프다
불행하다니 가슴 아프다
다시하자니 골치 아프다
첫사랑!
무소식이 희소식이다

## Time and Tide

It wasn't there before
the remorseful footprints
ah, am I old now

## 세월

예전에는 없었는데
돌아보면 아쉬움이
나 이제 늙었나 봐

## Hometown of New Gens

Hometown of the new gens
redevelopment section of Gangnam
not a poor village on the hillside

## 신세대 고향

신세대 고향
강남 재건축 단지
달동네도 아니고

## To Be Rich

Wanted to feel like a rich
counted the same $$ over and over
without sleeping all night long

## 부자가 되고 싶어

부자가 되고 싶어
돈 세고 또 세다
밤을 세웠다

## Handsome Grandpa

An autumn foliage leaf
more elegant than spring flowers
placed in between my diary pages
the handsome grandpa in nursing home

## 멋진 할아버지

잘 물들어진 단풍잎
봄꽃보다 아름다워
일기장에 꽂았다
양로원 가신 할아버지

## My Share

Destiny is given by God
also the wisdom is given
to overcome the destiny
of your life

## 나의 몫

신이 준 운명
극복의 지혜도 함께 받았다
비켜라 운명아

## Vagabond

Promised to each other
don't be a flock of wild geese
in the autumn sky
the monologue of vagabond

## 유랑인

너와 나는 말했지
가을하늘 기러기는
되지 말자고
유랑인의 독백

## Hollo Arirang

The wave of touching sound
made even more sentimental
echo of the island Dok-Do
Hollo Arirang

## 홀로 아리랑

너무 아름다워
더더욱 슬픈 소리
독도의 메아리
홀로 아리랑

## Time To Prepare To Die

Felt the number of days I lived
is greater than the days I may live
it's the time to prepare well dying

## 죽음을 준비할 때

살아온 날들이
살아갈 날들 보다
많다고 느껴질 때
죽음을 준비할 때

## I Am Old

One day suddenly
the sad past of my life
appeared to be more beautiful
the day before I got dementia

## 늙었구나

어느 날 갑자기
슬픔의 지난날이
아름답게 보였다
치매 걸리기 전날

## Husband and Wife

Husband and wife is (        )
a parenthesis opened and closed
placed her and him in it
that's a couple

## 남편과 아내

남편과 아내는 (     )
괄호 열고 괄호 닫고
그 속에 당신과 나
그것이 부부

## Dandelion

A life crushed and stepped on
the snow blanket kept me warm
while green leaves flat on the ground
delivered the message of spring
with yellow flowers blooming
then the white hairs blown away
me again to be a spore in the sky
it's only you, the dandelion

## 민들레

짓밟히며 살아온 잡초라지만
흰 눈은 따뜻이 덮어 주었다
열 손가락 파란 잎 땅에 펼치고
노란 꽃 피우며 봄소식 전하면
새하얀 머리카락 바람에 날려
또다시 홀씨로 일편단심 민들레

## A Sense of Futility

The body lives in today
the soul connects with future
the past is beautiful
it's the sense of futility

## 세월의 허무

몸은 오늘에 살고
영혼은 미래를 이으니
지나간 것은 아름다워라
세월이 허무한 이유

## Hope

The frog fallen
into a deep well
climbed up two steps
slided back one step
all day long
looking up the blue sky

## 희망

깊은 우물에 빠진
개구리 한 마리
두 발자국 올라오고
한 발 미끄러졌다
하루 종일
푸른 하늘을 보며

## The Wind of A Fan

The fan moved by the wind
or the wind moved by the fan
when the wind hesitated
stopped the fan and
the hand of grandpa

## 부채 바람

부채가 바람을 좇는지
바람이 부채를 움직이는지
바람이 서성거리니
부채도 할아버지 손도
함께 멈춰버렸다

## Love and Sins

Nominated for heaven
Quota to hell
Rich gets the quota
Nominations upon prayers

## 사랑과 죄악

천국은 추천제도
지옥은 분양제도
부자들은 분양받고
기도하면 추천받다

## God's Desire

The God's desire
given to us
made to taste the apple
and see the woman
is it an irony of God
or an oversight
why? if not
what would we be today
if that's not happened

## 신이 준 욕망

신이 준 욕망
사과 맛도 좋았고
이성도 눈에 보였다
이것은 장난인가?
신의 실수였을까?
아니면 왜
그러지 않았다면
오늘 우린 뭘 할까?

## A Wonderful Day

A wonderful day is
exchanging today
with beautiful memories
Then, I had a lot of dreams!

## 좋은 하루

좋은 하루는
오늘을
추억과 맞바꾸는 것
그땐 꿈도 많았지!

## A Word Not Said at The Last

Didn't say the word
till the last minutes
repeated alone over and over
I love you and I love you
saved it in heart
for the next life

## 끝내 못한 말

마지막 순간
끝내 하지 못한 말
혼자서 되뇌었다
사랑한다고
가슴에 묻었다
다시 만날 때까지

## Trust Yourself

Discover and trust yourself
as the saints have a past
the sinners have a future

## 자신을 믿어라

자신을 알고 믿어라
성인도 과거가 있고
죄인도 미래가 있다

## The New Year never Arrived

December 32, 33, 34... continued
As the waving gray hair in wind
never ending December

## 오지 않는 새해

12월 32일, 33, 34 ...
휘날리는 흰머리처럼
멈추지 않는 나의 12월

## Hometown

Wherever I go
there is no hometown
wherever I go
I see the hometown

Wherever I am looking for
there is no hometown
whenever in my heart
I always see the hometown

## 고향

가는 곳마다
고향은 없는데
가는 곳마다
고향이 보이더라

아무리 돌아봐도
고향은 없는데
내 마음에는 항상
고향이 보이더라

## Direction of Life

The clock lost in directions
is running around and around
without any dreams and goals
wondering as it's a vagabond
not knowing the importance of
direction than the speed in life

## 삶의 방향

방향을 잃은 시계
돌고 돌기만 한다
꿈도 목표도 없이
맴도는 유랑인처럼
삶에 중요한 것은
속도가 아니라
방향인 것을 모른다

## Love While With You

Out of sight
out of mind
love and hate
is only intimate
share the love and care
while you are with

## 있을 때 잘해

눈에서 멀어지면
마음도 멀어지랴
사랑도 미움도
가까이 있을 때
사랑하고 배려하라
곁에 있을 때

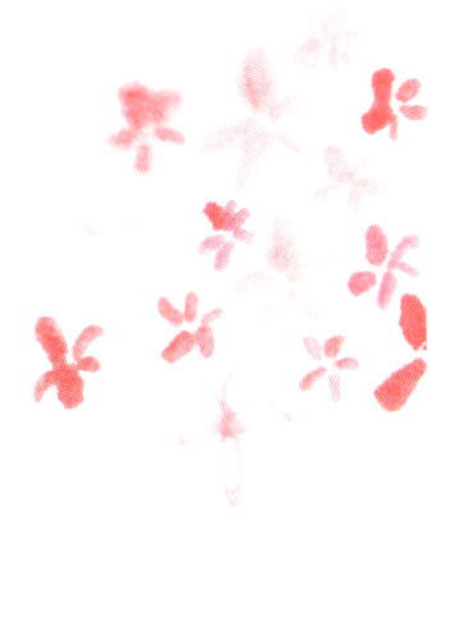

## Subject and Object

Loneliness
is the only subject
I can have for myself
Love
is the only object
I can not attain alone

## 주체와 대상

고독,
이 세상에서 혼자
가질 수 있는 것
사랑,
이 세상에서 혼자
가질 수 없는 것

## Tomorrow in Haze and Maze

Will live a day more
if it will make me happy
tomorrow in haze and maze
made me hesitate in heart

## 미로의 내일

행복할 수 있다면
더 살고 싶은 하루
망설이는 내 마음
미로의 내일인지라

## Ode to Chicken

Country chicken kokyo
colonel Yankee's KFC
love of Korean ChiMac
crazy Nipponno ToriSake
ode to country chicken

## 치킨 송시(頌詩)

촌닭들이 꼬끼오
양키들의 KFC
한국사람 치맥사랑
얼빠진 닛폰노 도리사케
촌닭들의 송시낭송

## Jealousy and Envy

Jealousy and envy
they are an expression of emotion
both are alike yet, different in directions
envy is toward to myself
jealousy is directed to others
Even the Saints struggle with it
controls the directions and focus

## 시기와 질투

시기와 질투는 감정의 표현
비슷하면서도 방향이 다르다
질투의 초점이 나에게 있다면
시기심은 언제나 남을 향한다
성인(聖人)도 번민하는 시기와 질투
방향과 초점을 바로 잡아라

## Believe in Miracles

Pray for miracles
if you believe it exists
miracles are a state of
against the law of nature
prayers are
the priming water of miracles

## 기적을 믿으려면

기도하라
기적을 믿는다면
기적은
자연의 법칙을
거스르는 행위지만
기도는
기적의 마중물이다

## Listen

The voice of God
listen up
listen in
listen for
listen out
primes to
transcend
self doubt

## 잘 들어라

신의 계시
잘 들어라
깊이 새겨들어라
귀담아들어라
주의해서 들어라
불신의 벽을
넘을 수 있을 때까지

## Turning of Sunflowers

Sunflowers move
east to west in the days
west to east at the nights
thought it follows the sunshine
it turns reversed in the night
what made it to turn back
a magic of coiling and uncoiling

## 돌고도는 해바라기

해바라기 꽃
낮엔 동에서 서쪽으로
햇볕 따라 돈다는데
햇빛 없는 밤중에는
서쪽에서 동쪽으로
어떻게 돌아왔지
감기고 풀리는 마술

## The Dates in History

625-419-516-0518
Telephone number, GI, or a personal ID?
it rings a bell to me
No, it's the resenting sound of machine gun,
the sound of marching soldiers

## 역사 속의 날들

625-419-516-0518
전화번호, 주민등록번호?
귀에 익은 숫자인데
아, 원한의 기관총 소리,
군인들의 발자국 소리

## Apartments on the Highways

High rise buildings
faced sideways on the road
lights on every floors
procession of cars on the highway

## 누워 있는 아파트

대로 위에 가로 누운
고층 아파트
층마다 불이 켜졌네
고속도로 자동차 행렬

## Pain of Going Over the Hills

Couldn't go over the hills
with the dying of hunger
sadden hills of spring famine

Gone over the hills
leaving my love behind
hateful hills of Arirang

## 넘기 힘든 고개들

배가 고파
넘지 못했다
한 맺힌 보릿고개

사랑 두고
넘어야했다
슬픔의 아리랑 고개

## The Fate of Shima

Hiroshima
Fukushima
What'shima
Nextshima
Up to U'shima

## 시마의 운명

히로시마
후쿠시마
뭐시마
넥스트시마
너에 달렸시마

## Strange Math

Nuclear arms
for me unlimited
for you nothing
strange principles of math

## 이상한 수학 공식

무서운 핵무기
나는 무제한
너는 무소유
이상한 수학공식

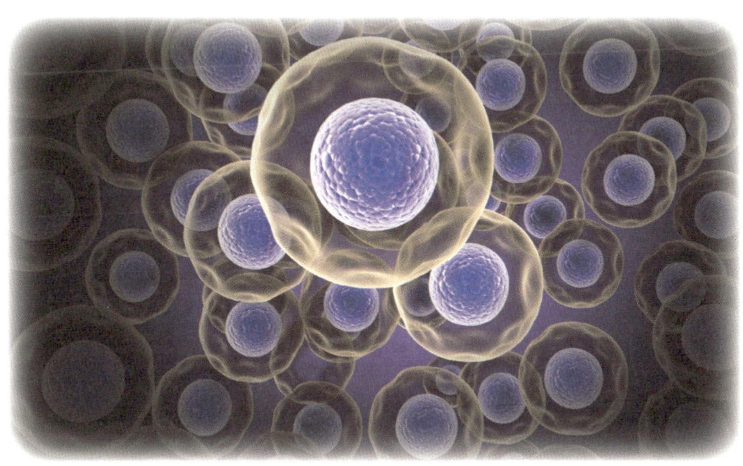

## Hurrah and Surrender

Both hands up and gave up
both hands up and shouted Hurrah in joy
both actions, something in common
hands up high in the both occations

## 항복과 승리

손들고 항복했다
손들고 만세 불렀다
두 가지의 공통점
두 손 높이 들었다

## War and Peace

Threat of Kim Jong Un
autocratic of super powers
the story of War and Peace
in Tolstoy's novel

## 전쟁과 평화

김정은의 공갈
열강들의 횡포
톨스토이 소설에 나오는
전쟁과 평화 이야기

## Full of Joy

Life is wonderful
Love is beautiful
Together is cheerful
Dream is fruitful
Blessed sna joyful today

## 가득찬 기쁨

인생은 경이롭고
사랑은 아름답고
함께하니 즐거워
꿈은 이루어지노라
축복과 기쁨의 오늘

## Unlucky Numbers 4 and 13

Don't like the number 4 and 13
in the East and in the West
thus a striking idea
the Friday 13th of April
Made a worldwide holiday

## 불운의 숫자 4와 13

서양은 13, 동양엔 4
모두 다 싫어하는 숫자
그래서 기발한 생각
4월 13일 금요일
전 세계 공휴일 만들다

## Feel Stomachache

Felt terrible stomachache
need the same medications
my cousin used to acquire properties

## 배가 아프다

배가 아프다
무슨 약이 좋을까?
사촌이 땅 산 약

## Remain in Peace

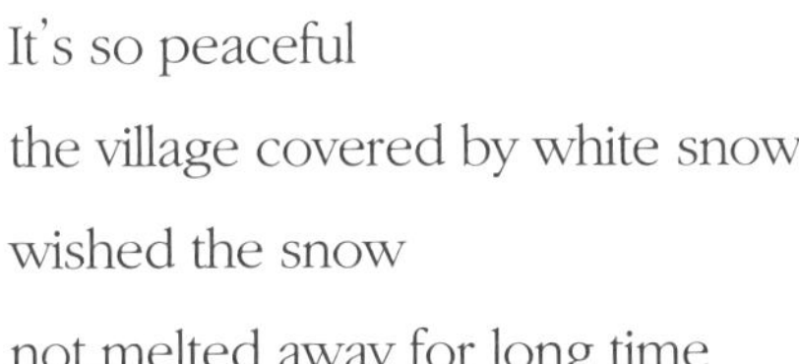

It's so peaceful
the village covered by white snow
wished the snow
not melted away for long time

## 평화가 함께

흰 눈 덮인 저 마을
평화가 함께 있었다
오랫동안 흰 눈이
녹지 않고 있었으면

## Enemies Befriended

Met the enemies where
could not escape from
a single log bridge,
the bitter enemies befriended
on the river in the same boat
go together and love
all is vanity in life

## 원수가 친구 되다

원수와 만나는
외나무다리
함께 탄 배 위에서
오월동주 친구 되다
함께 가라, 사랑하라
삶은 허무한 것이다

## Dreaming

Dream beyond a dream
you have never thought
Dream a journey
along the road none has sought

## 꿈을 꾸어라

꿈 넘어 꿈을 꾸어라
한 번도 상상하지 못한 것
인생 여로의 꿈을 꾸어라
아직 아무도 가지 않은 길

## Never Ending Turbulence

36 years of lasting regret
the heart sadly beat even today
80th anniversary of liberation
never ending ups and downs
turbulent times in divided fatherland

## 격동의 세월

한 많은 36년
오늘도 가슴 아프다
해방 된 지 80년
끝없는 격동의 세월
파란만장 분단의 조국

## The Beautiful Moon

On the beautiful moon
Lee Taebek under the olive tree*
wrote poems and read
not too many years ago
then Armstrong landed there
gone the tree and rabbit
it's the sad alien intrusion

## 아름다운 달나라

아름다운 둥근 달에
이태백과 계수나무
시를 읊고 놀던 달
오랜 옛날 아니련만
암스트롱 갔다 온 후
외계인에 짓밟힌 달
토끼와 계수나무 사라졌구나

---

* Olive tree on the moon is a symbol of peace. Although Gyesoo namoo in the legend is literary a cinnamon tree and Lee Taebek is a legendary character..

## Prayers

The clergy who met a tiger
shouted a petition prayer in scare
dear God please save my life

The tiger who received the food
happily presented a gratitude prayer
thanks God for the food provided.

Guess the one honored by God.

## 기도

호랑이를 만난 하느님의 제자
하느님 저를 제발 좀 살려 주세요
겁에 질려 청원기도 외쳤다

먹거리를 만나 은총받은 호랑이
하느님께 감사기도 드렸다
"저희에게 일용할 양식을 주시고"….

하느님이 먼저 들어 준 기도는

## Impeached Supreme Powers

Yeonsan Goon*
Kwanghae Goon
Guenhye Goon
Mot Duet Goon*
Dumber Goon

## 탄핵받은 최고권력

연산군
광해군
근혜군
못됐군
바보군

---

* Two Kings and one president were impeached in Korean history. Once a king is impeached the king is called "Goon" identifying the removed power and a demotion from king to prince level in national humiliation. Mot Duet Goon is a figurative expression of a bad person. The female (mot) duet represent monopolization of state affairs by two women, the president Park Geunhye lacking leadership and qualifications to be a president and her friend and traitor Choi Soonsil.

## The Cause of Death

The spirit of Cheonanham warship
the soul of Seweolho ferry liner
even the souls don't know
the cause of regrettable death
it's the ghost of Itewon

## 죽음의 원인

천안함 충정
세월호 영혼
영혼도 잘 모르는
한 맺힌 죽음의 원인
이태원 유령되다

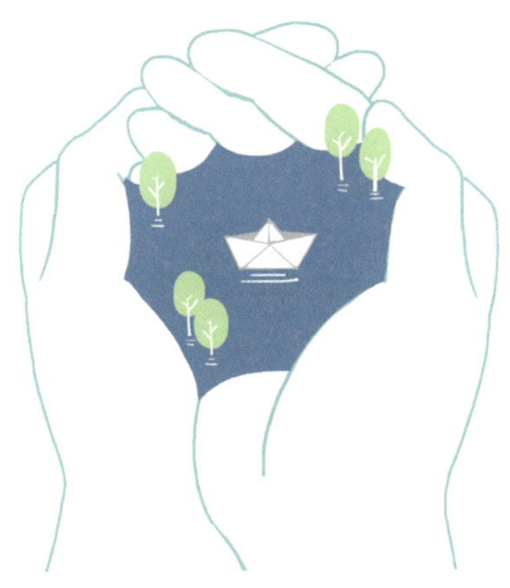

## One-Wing-Birds

A couple is like a pair of one-wing-birds
can only fly two together as one in pairs
some times in the journey of rough life
rested on the sleepy summer lake
the daydreaming one-wing-birds

## 비익조

부부는 비익조
혼자 날 수 없는 새
때로는 험난한 삶의 여정에
물결도 잠든 호수에 앉아
꿈 꾸는 비익조

## Blood is Thicker than the Water

Blood is thicker than the water
the same blood in the vein
of brothers and sisters
the flow of love of siblings
it's the love sometimes
it's a burden at the othertimes
and it is the shoulders
you can lean on sometimes
it pumps the blood all the times
it attacks the heart sometimes

## 물보다 진한 피

물보다 진한 피가 흐를 수 있음은
천륜으로 맺어진 형제의 가슴에
사랑과 연민을 따라 움직이는 것
때론 힘이 되고 때론 짐이 되어
심장을 뛰게 하고 멈추게 하는
물보다 진하고 붉은 사랑의 피
옹이 박혀 검게 탄 한 맺힌 피

## Proclamation

Victims or offenders
Pearl Harbor and Hiroshima
monologue of the victors and defeated
a story of war and peace

## 성명서

피해자와 가해자
진주만과 히로시마
승자와 패자의 독백
전쟁과 평화 이야기

## The Wave of Me Too

The wave of “me too” movement,
she too and he too
loved each other at the one point
romance for me, adultery for you
money talks, money makes not to talk

## 미투 바람

미투 운동의 물결
그 여자도, 그 남자도
한때 서로 사랑했던가
아니, 내로남불 이라고 해
돈은 말도 하고 입도 막고

## Windflower

A softly bloomed windflower
next to grandma's tomb
her troublesome life
made it to bow the head
the hardship of her life
made it a hunchback

## 할미꽃

할머니 무덤 옆에
살짝 핀 할미꽃
지나간 세월이
너무 무거워
고개를 떨구고
허리 굽혔네

## What shall I Do

When the wind touches sea
it wakes up the wave
when the wind shakes trees
it creates sound
when you rock my heart
what shall I do

## 나는 어쩌나

바람이 물결을 흔들면
파도가 일고
바람이 나무를 흔들면
소리를 낸다
당신이 내 마음 흔들면
나는 뭘하지

## Peace on Earth

The sky and sea
kissed at the end of horizon
once the earth is vanished
the peace of the world is breathing
and covered by the dense fog

## 이 땅에 평화

하늘과 바다가 맞닿은
수평선 끝자락
지구는 사라져 버렸다
안개 자욱한 저 너머
평화가 숨 쉬는 그곳

## To Be As Is

Share the experience of pain
without fabricated messages
just true me to you
relate the heart to heart
you and I are a trusted friend

## 있는 그대로

겪었던 아픔을 나누며
꾸밈없는 메시지
가슴에서 가슴으로
나를 너에게 전하면
너와 나는 진정한 친구

## The Biggest Tragedy of Life

Who never loved by anyone is
the biggest tragedy of one's life
one doesn't know how to love is
who was never loved by anyone
love is such a sad and painful legacy

## 삶의 가장 큰 비극

인생의 가장 큰 비극
사랑받지 못하는 것
사랑받지 못했기에
사랑할 줄 모르는 것
슬프고 아픈 사랑의 유산

## Things Left Traces

The wind shook trees
the sunlight made shadow
as the love pumped heart
left many traces in heart

## 흔적을 남기는 것들

바람은 나뭇잎을 움직이고
햇빛은 그림자를 만든다
심장을 뛰게 하는 사랑은
가슴에 흔적을 남긴다

## The Road Never Traveled

The tail wind pushed to go fast
walked along the sunlight in front
no shadow could be seen
I am the first one
walking on the road never traveled
it's the far and rough road of destiny
need to be conquered in life.

## 아무도 가지 않은 길

바람이 밀어주니
빨리 갈 수 있었다
태양을 안고 가면
그림자는 보이지 않았다
아무도 가지 않은
처음 가는 길
내가 넘고 가야 할
멀고 험한 길

## Loneliness

She is gone
who saw the flowers blooming
together with me in the backyard
the red floral leaves today
seen by the lonely eyes
silently falling on the ground
it made to lower my head
to hide the tears of longing

## 외로움

뒤뜰에 핀 꽃 함께 보던
당신이 떠나버린 그날
혼자 보는 외로운 꽃
말없이 떨어져 버렸다
그리움의 눈물 감추려
고개 떨구는 꽃과 나

## Moon Kyeong Hills

Left a sentiment over the Moon Kyeong hills
on the way to take the state exam "Kwageo"
passed the Kwageo with honor
stoped by again at the Moon Kyeong hills
on the way back to home
looked for the short love
to make a long lasting memory
of Moon Kyeong Hills

## 문경새재

정을 두고 넘었다
과거 길목 문경새재
장원급제 귀향길에
다시 찾은 문경새재
짧은 인연 오래도록
두고 넘은 문경새재

## A Promise Filled With Soul

You have it too
a word, one never said at last
can't be erased over the long time
neither burned and nor made ash
the promise, the phoenix of soul

## 영혼을 담은 약속

누구나 가슴에 담고있는
끝내 하지 못한 말 한마디
세월이 지나도 지워지지 않는
태워도 태워도 재가 되지 않는
바로 그 약속, 영혼의 불사조

## Not an Easy Life

The ambitions given by God
can never fully be filled
it only made all the things
and the tenor of life
never be easy

## 쉽지 않은 삶

세상만사 인생살이
쉽지 않은 이유는
채워도 채워도 끝이 없는
신이 준 욕망 때문에

# East-West Epic

*Surround-Sound Poetry with no Boundary*

## The School on The Road

Traveling is a moving school on the road
we happen to meet a destiny of new acquaintances,
and come to learn the life and the direction of life

Learned how to love and share a deep impression
how to forgive and re conciliate between us
we came to learn the skill of planning our life
both a real enjoyment and happiness

Life is traveling through the road,
the road with a moving school for life
where people can learn and conduct
a simple but commanding and dignified life.

## 길 위의 학교

여행은 길 위의 움직이는 학교
운명과도 같은 새로운 만남과
인생과 삶의 방향을 배운다

사랑하고 감동을 나누는 법과
용서하고 화해하는 법도 배운다
인생을 새롭게 설계하는 기술과
진정한 기쁨과 행복도 배우게 된다

단순하면서도 당당하게 사는 법을
배울 수 있는 길 위의 학교를 따라
우리는 여행을 떠나고 있는 것이다

## Tears, A Language without Words

Tears are a wet language
delivers pure and plain messages
more than the words can do

Tears flow from the deep heart
and connect the past and future
though the past causes tears to flow
the future afterward stops the tears

Tears are a non-spoken language
tears are a promise with future
as it is a language of "desire"

## 눈물은 말 없는 언어

눈물은 젖어있는 언어
눈물은 순수하고 꾸밈없이
말보다 더 많은 것을 전한다

눈물은 가슴에서 흘러나오고
과거와 미래를 연결하게 한다
살아온 날들이 눈물을 쏟게 했지만
살아갈 날들은 눈물을 멈추게 한다

눈물은 말 없는 언어
눈물은 미래와의 약속이며
눈물은 "바람"의 언어이니까

## Divorce

The life without you
can not be in existence
I will be gone together
on the day of your death
promised to each other
with the flimsy tongues

Nurtured the love for you
for the happiness tomorrow
took the sacrifice today
at the place under your shade
is for me to rest

Shattered dreams of ours
at a point of witnessing
the untruth of our promise
I am going to my way
you to your way
don't ask to each other
when did I say that.

At the end of
every thing is for myself
wished to exist and
to be accomplished
all things just said with
your name borrowed.

## 이혼

그대 없는 세상은
존재하지 않는다고
당신이 죽는 날엔
나도 함께 갈 것이라며
얄팍한 혀끝으로
함께 약속했었지

당신을 위해 산다며
사랑을 키워 왔지요
내일의 행복을 위해
오늘의 희생을 감내하며
당신의 그늘 밑이
내가 쉴 곳이라 했었지

산산이 깨어진 꿈은
모든 것이 거짓임을
확인하는 갈림길에서
너는 너대로 나는 나대로
언제 그런 말을 했느냐고
물어 무엇해

결국은 모든 것이

나를 위하여

있어 주고 되어주길

바라는 마음

그대의 이름 빌려

말 한 것뿐인데

## Shadow Can Not Be Seen

The philosopher said that
the shadow of yourself can't be seen
when you walk toward sunshine.

I saw the flashing light toward me
passing through the dark tunnel
of wind-blown dust
while searching for the meaning
of life and planting dreams,
who restlessly running forward
could not see the shadow of own

That's the way brought me today.

## 보이지 않는 그림자

태양을 안고 가는 사람에게는
그림자가 보이지 않는다고 하였다!

길고 컴컴한 풍진의 터널을 지나
섬광이 비치는 길을 찾았다
인생을 캐고 희망을 꿈꾸며
쉴 새 없이 앞만 보고 달리는
나의 그림자는 보이지 않았다

오늘의 내가 여기까지 오는 날

## Be a Diamond

To transform charcoal to diamond
high pressure is applied
it remains as charcoal soots
if it couldn't resist to high pressure

The pain is a process of pressure
applied to charcoal transform
to a diamond
apply the pressure to transform
the charcoal of your heart
to a pure diamond
not to remain as charcoal soots

## 다이아몬드가 되어라

숯은 강한 압력을 받아야
다이아몬드로 바뀐다
고도의 압력을 견디지 못하면
숯은 숯검정으로 남는다

고통은 숯을 다이아몬드로
바꾸는 압력의 과정일지니
내 가슴에 잠재해 있는 숯을
다이아몬드로 바꾸어라
그대가 숯검정으로 머물지 않게

## Loneliness and Fear

When the tough life is lonely
walk looking the road you just passed
you will see the shadow
coming along with you

When the fear and dread attacks you
walk looking the road you just passed
you will the footprints
walking along with you

Felt the life is tiring and uneasy
sit back and close your eyes
to see the smile of the past

## 고독과 두려움

삶이 힘들고 외로울 때면
뒤를 보고 걸어라
그림자라도 볼 수 있게

무섭고 두려움이 찾아오면
뒤를 보며 걸어라
발자국이 함께 갈 수 있게

삶이 지치고 어려울 때면
눈을 감고 앉아 쉬어라
추억이 미소 지을 수 있게

## Be a Happy Man

However it may be a tough life today
happy man is who keep the composure

Knowing the grace rather than disaffection
happy man is who doesn't forget gratitude

Knowing how to understand rather scolding
happy man is who can smile with love

Struggled and wriggled to find happiness
Happy man is who thanks to own happiness

## 행복한 사람

오늘의 삶이 아무리 어려워도
마음의 여유를 가지면 행복한 사람

섭섭함보다 베풀어 준 은혜
감사하고 잊지 않으면 행복한 사람

나무라기보다 이해하는 마음으로
웃을 줄 아는 사람 행복한 사람

행복을 찾으려고 발버둥 쳤지만
내가 가진 행복에 감사하는 사람

## Erasing Past

What should I erase with
if I get an eraser which
can erase only one of my past.

The time in the past

## 과거를 지울 수 있는 지우개

단 하나의 과거를 지울 수 있는
지우개가 나에게 주어진다면
나는 무엇을 지울까?

지나간 세월

## Song of Birds

Song of birds sitting high and low
on the telephone wire and poles
drawn parallel lines and dots
like a music sheet in the blue sky
songs hugging the lyrics of time
echoed around the green mountains
time and tide flew away with the birds
once the concerto was over

## 새들의 노래

푸른 하늘에 평행선 그린
전깃줄 따라 점을 찍고
높고 낮게 나란히 앉아
악보를 그리고 노래하는 새
세월을 가사에 담아
청산에 메아리치는 협주
새들의 합창이 끝나면
세월도 새와 함께 날아가노라

## Arirang Moonlight Sonata

Arirang, Arirang, Hollo Arirang
riding on the wave of moonlight
it's the shadow of my love
who deserted me in vain
Arariyo

The handsome face of my dear
disappearing in far away
he is the one who is heartlessly
going over the hill of Arirang

Don't you dare to leave
the beautiful woman in sigh
the one who left her
got blisters on the feet
before gone not too far

## 아리랑 월광곡

달빛 파도를 타고
아리랑, 아리랑, 홀로 아리랑
무심히 버리고
떠난 님의 그림자
불러보는 아라리오

저 멀리 사라지는
아름다운 그 모습
뒤돌아보지 않고
넘어가는 아리랑 고개

한숨 짓는 이 여인
어이 두고 떠나시나
날 버리고 가시는 님
십 리도 못가 발병 나요

## Flowing River As One

Together, you and me
as a community of two lives
like the cloud formed as one
sometimes covers the sun
makes rain and snow
turns into river again
shattered by the rocks
falls at the cliff

Together, you and me
flowing river as one
in the ever-changing river of life
stopped together in silence
arrived at the silvery ocean

## 하나 되어 흐르는 강

사랑하는 부부는
두 생명이 하나 된 공동체

부부가 함께 가는 길은
하나가 된 구름이
때로는 태양을 가리고
눈과 비를 내리며
다시 하나인 강물이 되어
돌부리를 만나 부서지고
절벽을 만나 떨어진다

너와 나는 함께
변화무쌍한 인생의 강물에
하나 되어 흘러가는 부부
함께 은빛 바다에 다다라
침묵 속에 멈출 때까지

## The World And The Beyond

Nine months of hesitation
on the way to this world
ninety years of probation
the way to the world beyond
nine hundreds years purgatory
the way of discipline to the heaven
nine thousands Hades in haze and maze
ninety thousands miles to the heaven
to the world from the world beyond
is no way for a transfer
gone there soon or late
no way for no body to return

## 이승과 저승

구 개월 유예기간
이 세상 오는 길
구십 년 집행유예
저 세상 가는 길
구백 년 연옥 기간
천국 가는 수련길
구천을 헤맨 시간
황천 가는 험한 길
구만리 길 저승에선
환승 되지 않는 길
한 번 가면 누구도
돌아오지 않는 길

## Nohgohjiree – Ideology of The President Noh

An eagle trained by the bird-trainer
can not fly in the vast sky
only performs tricks with circus troupe
a skylark singing and piercing the sky
will only die depressingly
if it's reared in a cage.

In the roughly devastated wilderness
with the dreams of peace and prosperity
between North and South, East and West
an ambitious skylark, the Nohgohjiree

Breathing hard and flying harshly
passing through the tunnel of Korean history
and for a moment in the world of ordinary people
flapping its' broken wings
climbed up to the edge of Mt. Bonghwa
at last it was not to be seen any more

It's said that the spring will be on this land
when the skylark is singing in the high sky

now, over the land ever frozen
the Nohgohjiree flying around blue sky
with piercing and singing its' ideology
Nohgohjiree sadly echoed today

## 노고지리(盧考之理) - 고 노무현 대통령 추모 시

조련사가 길들인 독수리는
광활한 하늘을 날지 못하고
곡예단과 함께 재주를 부린다
하늘을 찢고 우는 노고지리는
새장에 가두고 키우려 하면
아예 죽어버리고 만다

험상이 돋친 쑥대밭 속에서
시대의 동서와 남북을 관통해
숨 가삐 그리고 모질게 달려온
풍운의 노고지리

역사의 터널을 지나
"사람 사는 세상" 속에서 한순간
부러진 날개를 푸드덕거리며
봉화산 끝자락에 오르더니
끝내 보이지 않았다

종달새, 노고지리가 울면
이 땅에도 봄이 온다 했었는데
봄이 오지 않는 동토 위에

하늘을 찢고 우는 노고지리여
가슴에 메아리치는 노고지리여

## The First Promise

The first promise is
the first resolutions made with myself
it's just pure and beautiful
it's not a subject for change
first promise will be shined
at the time it's harvested.

## 초심

초심은
내가 처음 마음먹은
자신과의 약속
변심의 대상이 아닌
순결하고 아름다운 것
더욱더 빛나는 순간은
초심이 결실을 맺었을 때

## Birds Without Wings

The wind rolled the leaves
to make the birds without wings
the clouds moved the sky
to flow the storm of tears

The birds without wings
fell and roll on the ground
wanted to fly together
wanted to cry together
the birds of fallen leaves
the birds without wings

## 날개 없는 새

바람은 나뭇잎을 흔들어
날개 없는 새를 만들고
구름은 하늘을 움직여
눈물을 흘리게 만든다

땅 위에 굴러떨어진
날개 없는 새
함께 날고 싶었다
함께 울고 있었다
날지 못해 떨어진
날개 없는 낙엽 새

## Prayers

It's not the way I prayed for
I am satisfied with what I am today

It's not the way I prayed for
I am satisfied with what I have today

It's not the way I prayed for
I am satisfied with where I am today

It's not the way I prayed for
I am happy with my family today

Thanks to God rather than asking
I am happy with presenting
prayer of thanks to God

## 기도하는 마음

내가 기도한 대로는 아니지만
지금의 내 모습에 만족합니다.

내가 기도한 대로는 아니지만
지금의 내가 가진 것에 만족합니다.

내가 기도한 대로는 아니지만
지금의 내 위치에 만족합니다.

내가 기도한 대로는 아니지만
지금의 우리 가족과 가정에 행복합니다.

청원하기보다는 감사해야겠기에
오늘도 감사기도 드리며 행복합니다.

## The Weed

The winter weed in brown
as it's hibernating hiding the face
down on the frozen field
waiting for the days of
wake up and stand up
to put on the green dress
to change the dress of time

I, the person insensitive to time
put the thick winter coat away
but, the dress of heart
remained the same as the past winter

Oh Lord,
the weeds, even for just a moment
would be a mentor of the life.

## 잡초

한겨울 잡초는 제 몸을 말려
얼굴을 가리고 동면하듯 누워 지낸다

오로지 몸을 세울 그 날을 위해
겉을 감추고
때가 되면 언제나
푸른 옷을 입는다
세월의 옷을 갈아입는다

세월에 무딘 우리는
한겨울의 옷은 갈아입어도
정녕 마음의 옷은
지난겨울 그 옷 그대로구나

하여
잡초여, 당신은 잠시
나의 스승이 되었다.

## Migrated Flowers

Cosmos flowers which left the fatherland
bloomed in the spring of a foreign land
forgotten the season of blooming
morning glories tired with the long flight
to a new land across the Pacific
confused with the time changes
bloomed in the daytime

Chrysanthemums bloomed
in the early spring,
and azaleas in the fall
not in the seasons as usual
you and I both confused
at a foreign land soaked in nostalgia

You and I who left the hometown
now, in a hazy directions and times
spent long time at the other side of the world
morning glories still blooming in the day time
at a ever strange place.

## 낯선 곳에 핀 꽃

고향을 잃은 코스모스는
계절을 잊은 채 봄에 피었고
먼 여행에 지친 나팔꽃이
시차를 모르고 대낮에 피었다.

초봄에 국화가 만발하고
철쭉이 가을을 물들이면
너와 나는 정신을 잃었다
향수의 슬픔에 젖어

고향을 잃은 너와 나는
시간도 방향도 흐릿한
긴 세월 지구의 반대편
낯선 곳에 낮에 핀 나팔꽃

## Light and Salt

Salt
seasons and makes the food tasty
by only melting its' own body

Light
brightens and shines the road
when its' own body is burned

Oh Lord,
Salt and Light,
you are the mentor in life

## 빛과 소금

소금은
내 몸을 녹여
맛을 내고 간을 맞춘다

빛은
내 몸을 태워
빛을 내고 길을 밝힌다

하여 나의 스승은
빛과 소금

## The Tree and Fallen Leaves

Is it the tree let the leaves to leave
is it the leaves left the tree behind
who misses whom more
longed for son, missed for mom

## 나무와 낙엽

나무가 나뭇잎을 떠나게 한 것인가
낙엽이 나무를 홀로 두고 간 것인가
누가 누구를 더 그리워하고 있을까
엄마가 그리워, 자식이 보고파

## Passion of Geese

Across the Pacific Ocean
two nests of geese were built
one nest for the children at this side
an old nest of my mom at the other side
flew with embracing love and nostalgia
in the heart of lonely geese

## 기러기 연정

태평양 가로질러
두 개의 둥지 둔 기러기
이쪽은 아기 둥지
저쪽은 엄마 둥지
외로운 기러기
가슴에 품고 날랐다
사랑과 향수

## Debt to Parental Love

Nothing has been changed
even the daughter became the mom
love to the children, heart of parents
one never understood the heart
the depth of mother's love

## 부모님 은혜

딸이 엄마 되어도
변하지 않는 것은
자식 사랑 부모 마음
너는 몰라라 그 정성
모정의 깊이

# Lyrics of East Transcend to West

*Poetry with Personal Touches*

## Two Fatherlands

I have two glorious fatherlands
on each side of the Pacific Ocean,
one gave the birth to me
the other brought me up today

My soul always remember the fatherlands
one gave me the birth
and the other one where my flesh is nurtured
and made me to feel honored.
There was the old fatherland at night
here is the new fatherland in daytime,
I always belong to both fatherlands

I sang "God bless America" at the place
where I am with my fatherland of today
I hummed "Arirang while drunk on Soju
when longing for my fatherland of yesterday

Never forgot the old fatherland, even today
where my forefathers were buried
Love the new fatherland, now and forever
where the place away from home
became a new homeland of mine.

## 두 개의 조국

나에게는 두 개의 조국이 있다
태평양을 사이에 두고
나를 낳아준 조국과
나를 키워준 조국이 있다

마음은 언제나 낳아준 조국에
몸은 오늘도 길러준 조국에
밤에는 내 조국 낮에는 이 나라
언제나 나에겐 두 개의 조국

오늘의 조국과 함께한 자리에서
"갓 블레스 아메리카"를 불렀고
어제의 조국이 그리울 때면
소주에 취하여 "아리랑"을 불렀다

나는 잊지 않았노라, 오늘도
조상님 뼈 묻힌 나의 옛 조국
나는 사랑하노라, 영원히
타향도 고향 되는 오늘의 조국

## Wanted To Be a Township Clerk

Failed I to be a Myeon Seogi*
⟨a township clerk⟩ in my hometown
the simple wish of my father
it's a life time burden to me
even today questioning why not

My dear father knew
the happiness of being with family
his wish was so simple one
due to sorrow past of uneasy life

Just wanted me be next to him
need not be rich and famous
didn't I know the meaning of his wish
why I couldn't be a Myeon Seogi
in my hometown.

---

* a low ranking clerk in the township office

## 면서기도 못된 아들

시골 면서기도 못된 아들은
아버지의 소박한 소원을
받들지 못한 마음의 부담에
오늘도 물음표를 찍고 있었다

혼자가 아닌 가족의 행복이
무엇인지를 아시는 아버지는
큰 것을 바라지도 않으셨다
힘들게 살아온 삶이 서러워

커다란 부와 명예도 원함 없이
그저 당신 곁에 있어 달라고
그 뜻을 모르지도 않았지만
나는 왜 면서기가 못되었을까

## Seaweet Soup

Seaweed soup
mother's tears is boiled in it
the longing of my family
melted in the seaweed soup
the seaweed soup mom cooked
for the birthday of her son
who left home and gone far away

# 미역국

엄마의 눈물로
끓인 미역국
가족의 그리움이
녹은 미역국
멀리 간 아들의
생일 미역국

## Longing Elder Brother

My elder brother,
the pillar of our family went to Seoul
my elder brother, the idol of our family
went to West Germany
missed him so much and sang the song
"thinking of my elder brother"
mom and dad cried in silence

Cried when received a letter from him
waited for the day of returning to home
mom offered the seaweed soup on his birthday
and consecrating bowl of blessed water

The fate of being brothers and sisters
lasted long time hiding the attachment
the time gone in sorrow is too much to take
sang the song "thinking of my brother"

## 오빠 생각

기둥이신 우리 오빠 서울 가셨네
나의 우상 우리 오빠 서독 가셨네
오빠가 그리워 "오빠 생각" 부르면
엄마도 아빠도 소리 없이 우셨네

기다리던 오빠 소식 기뻐 울었고
돌아오실 그 날만 기다리면서
오빠 없는 생일상에 올린 미역국
정화수 담아놓고 빌던 어머니

오빠와 동생으로 맺어진 인연
아쉬움을 뒤로하고 살아온 세월
한 많은 그 세월이 너무 서러워
오늘도 "오빠 생각" 불러봅니다.

## When the Magpie Cries

The magpies cried sadly
when I made a long-awaited visite
to the mom's graveyard
to recollect the love of my mom
saying that your daughter is here

The magpies cried sadly
as it's conveying for my sadness
to the sunny graveyard
where my mom is resting in peace
asked why did you go so early.

The mom magpies and kid magpies
cried together whenever
I made a visit my mom's graveyard
saying I miss you, mom
I love you, my daughter Yong Ah

Now, my mom is gone and

my dad is also gone

and I am a mom for many years

the magpie asked to me

do you know the heart of mom

* *The legend says that magpie, a bird with black and white wings, smaller than a crow is a messenger delivering good news and indicating someone long awaited person will be coming to see you when it cries and flies around you.*

## 까치가 울면

모정의 사랑 찾으려고
모처럼 찾아본 어머님 산소
까치는 울고 있었다
딸이 찾아 왔노라고

양지바른 선산에
잠드신 어머니
딸의 슬픔 대신해
왜 그리 일찍 가셨냐며
까치는 슬피 울고 있었다

엄마 까치 새끼 까치
울고 있었다
내가 갈 때마다
엄마가 보고 싶어
내 딸이 보고 싶어

엄마도 가고 아빠도 가고
이제 내가 엄마 된 지
벌써 수십 년
까치는 물었다
이제야 부모 마음 너도 알리라…….

## Hometown

Wherever I go, there's no hometown
wherever I go, I can see the hometown
where the skeleton of my forefathers is buried
where I played with my childhood friends
no matter how I may look around
no where is the hometown can be seen,
my heart always find the hometown

Wherever I go, there is no hometown
wherever I go, I can see the hometown
hometown is like my mother
drawing her face in the sleepless nights
no matter how I may look around
no where the hometown can be seen
my heart always find the hometown

## 고향

가는 곳마다 고향은 없는데
가는 곳마다 고향이 보이더라
조상님 뼈가서 묻힌 그 고향
강아지 동무들과 놀던 내 고향
아무리 돌아봐도 고향은 없는데
내 가슴에는 항상 고향이 보이더라

가는 곳마다 고향은 없는데
가는 곳마다 고향이 보이더라
고향은 언제나 나의 어머니
그 모습 못 잊어 잠을 설치며
아무리 돌아봐도 고향은 없는데
내 가슴에는 항상 고향이 보이더라

## Dreams of HanGang Blossomed at The River of Rhein

You here, I there faraway
on the day I departed Korea
when I pledged myself to transfer
"the Miracle of Rhein" to Hangang.
the poverty of national income $72
was all that inherited from our fatherland.

You became a farmer, I became a miner
just as a means of livelihood,
you at the edge of our hometown,
I under the sky of an alien country

In Germany in the mines and hospitals
we learned the Miracle of Rhein
intensely devoting our youth
dreamt the miracle of the Hangang
and nourished the hope of Seoul

Sent the fruits of dreams and hope
to our fatherland to the last penny
the awaited news you sent to me

is that of an express highway being built
from Seoul all the way to Busan
and that of soaring smoke
of the factory chimney day and night

Today I again shed the tears of joy
at the riverside of Rhein

Witnessing Hyundai autos on Autobahn
Samsung TV in German Living rooms
I saw and knew that
"my dream of Hangang
blossomed at the riverside of Rhein
was never in vain.

## 라인강 변에 피운 한강의 꿈

너는 여기서 나는 멀리 저기서
라인강의 기적을 한강에 피우려고
다짐하며 떠나던 그 날
국민 소득 72달러의 가난이
우리가 받은 유산의 전부였다

너와 나는 먹고살기 위해
너는 농부가 되고 나는 광부가 되었지
고향의 언저리에서 이방의 하늘 밑에서
내게 라인강의 기적을 보여준 독일
광산에서 병원에서 젊음을 불태우며
한강의 기적을 꿈꾸었고
서울의 희망을 키워 왔었다

꿈과 희망의 열매를 한 줌도
남김없이 조국으로 보내면
네가 보내준 기다리던 그 소식
서울에서 부산까지 고속도로가 뚫리고
공장 굴뚝에는 밤낮없이 연기가 난다고

나는 오늘 다시 라인강 변에서

기쁨의 눈물을 흘렸다

현대 자동차가 아우토반을 달리고
독일의 안방을 차지한 삼성 TV
내 젊음을 아낌없이 바치며 그때
라인강 변에 피웠던 한강의 꿈이
나는 보았다, 결코 헛되지 않았음을

## To My Beloved Seong Ah

Seong Ah,
Do you know I love you
Do you know I am calling you
why don't you answer me
why don't you even look at me
why don't you say a word

You not knowing your checkered destiny
and scared of stormy life
decided to live without saying a word
decided to stare only the void sky
Seong Ah, what should I do
what's mom can do for you

My life with you
trusting me like it's your fate
even the destiny of ill-fated
is given to you by God
I worry you die ahead of me
and I worry I die ahead of you

Said that the life is short
Looking forward to meet you in heaven
without any tears and sadness
we will share the words and love
with you not disabled body and soul
over the night and over the day
with me, the mom…….

## 사랑하는 성아에게

성아!
내가 너를 사랑하는데
내가 너를 불러보는데
돌아보지도 않고
너는 왜 대답이 없니
왜 아무 말도 하지 않느냐?

기구한 운명도 모른 채
험악한 삶이 두려워
말없이 살겠다며
허공만 쳐다보면
성아! 엄마는 어떻게
엄마는 어떡해

너와 함께 사는 내 인생
나만 믿고 사는 네 팔자
짓궂은 운명도 하느님이
정해 주셨다지만
네가 먼저 갈까 걱정
내가 먼저 갈까 걱정

인생은 짧은 삶이라니
천국에서 만나는 날엔
눈물도 슬픔도 없이
나누지 못한 정과 말
장애인이 아닌 몸과 맘으로
밤새우며 나누자
엄마와 함께

## The River Flows Only at The Night

The river in dreams,
with peace and love
only flows in the nights
under the shining moon
or even in complete darkness

In the starry nights
I am flowing with the river
making curves and turns
dreaming hometown memories
the river flows only in the nights

The river embracing
never forgettable compassion
in a quiet waves
flows only in the nights

The river stops flowing
not making noise and wave
in the daytimes
preoccupied with struggle for life
and no time for dreaming
flows only in the nights.

## 밤에만 흐르는 강

강물은 꿈을 꾸며
유유히 흐른다
달 밝은 밤에도
어두운 밤에도

별 많은 밤에는
나와 함께 굽이굽이
고향의 꿈을 꾸며
밤에만 흐르는 강

잊을 수 없는 정
아름답게 담고서
잔잔한 파도 속에
밤에만 흐르는 강

낮에는 삶에 바빠
돌아볼 틈 없으니
물결도 멈춰버린
밤에만 흐르는 강

## Three Glasses of Wine

Felt a sense of intimacy
by exchanging a glass of wine
at a strange place away from home
and approached me as friend
when shared the second glass of wine

Accepted the third glass of wine
shared much of time together
talking about dreams and hope
peace with you and me in comfort

It's called a "relationship
even if the edges of sleeves grazed
in the inevitable everyday life
which is neither coincidence
nor ill-fated relationship
I wish to have friends who
can share three glasses of wine
next time and next

## 석 잔의 술

낯선 곳에서 한 잔의 술을 나누면
서로 친근감을 느낀다
두 잔의 술을 함께 나누면
당신은 나의 친구로 다가온다

내가 권하는 석 잔의 술을
받는 그 자리의 당신과 나는
꿈을 나누고 희망과 평화가 있었다
이미 많은 시간을 함께 했었다

옷자락만 스쳐도 인연이라지만
악연도 우연도 아닌 필연의 삶에서
다음에 그리고 또 다음에도
석 잔의 술을 함께 나눌 수 있는
친구를 더 많이 갖고 싶다.

## Mom's Birthday

Holding blind mom with one hand
three quarter coins in the other hand
the boy stopped in front of a restaurant

The boy and mom chased out of door
fell on cold street and crying
mom comforted the son
the son said, mom, it's your birthday
Only three quarters in my hand.

## 엄마의 생일

장님의 손을 잡은 소년은
25전짜리 동전 세 개를
다른 한 손에 쥐고
어느 식당 앞에 멈춰섰다

쫓겨 난 소년이 울음 속에
넘어진 차가운 땅바닥
장님은 아들을 끌어 앉았다
엄마, 오늘이 엄마 생일인데
25전짜리 동전 세 개뿐

## Sadness in Life

When sadness approached me
accept it without resentment
the sadness is part of our life
sadness delivered joy as bonus
and teaches the preciousness of joy
while the sadness circles around me

## 슬픔

슬픔이 찾아 왔을 땐
원망하지 말고 받아드려라
슬픔 없이 살 수 없는 세상
슬픔은 기쁨을 덤으로 주는것
기쁨의 소중함 알려주려고
오늘도 슬픔은 내곁에 있었다

## Life is a Market Place

A successful man in fortunate life
is a man how to sell all in life
sell the goods, sell the idea
sell the smile and fluent tongue
sell the philosophy and faith in life
buy and sell to each other
and cheat and be cheated
life is a process of selling and buying
a market place of unlimited contest

## 인생은 장터

잘 살고 성공한 사람은
세일즈를 잘할 줄 아는 사람
물건을 팔고 아이디어를 팔고
철학과 믿음을 팔고
미소와 능변을 팔고
모든 것을 팔고 사고,
서로가 속고 속이는 삶은
서로가 팔고 사는 과정
무한경쟁의 장터에서

## Know Yourself

To be successful in life
need to know who you are:
hope in the persons love the spring
mature in the persons love the autumn
high ambition in the persons love mountains
warm heart in the persons love the sea
humanity in the persons respect Confucius
faith in the persons believe in God
Success to the persons who
trust and know yourself

## 자신을 알자

자신을 알아야 성공할 수 있다
봄을 좋아하는 사람은 희망을
가을을 사랑하는 사람은 성숙을
산을 좋아하는 사람은 높은 뜻을
바다를 찾는 사람은 넓은 마음을
공자를 존경하는 사람은 참된 인성을
신을 믿는 사람에게는 믿음을
자신을 알고 믿는 사람은 성공을

## The Father

My father is the one
I couldn't be close to him
who shared love in silence
was a compass in life
for the right direction of life
the empty feeling is too much
to take when he left me

## 아버지

아버지는 나에게
다가서기 어려운 존재였다
말없이 사랑을 보내고
나침반으로 바른길을
가르쳐주신 아버지
당신이 떠나신 자리
너무 큰 빈자리

## The Teachings of Frog

The frog
made a statement
after finishing of a big jump
I can jump so high
a foolish creature
knows itself

The humanbeings
make an arrogant statement
before making any jump
made a confession
after the failed attempt
the pride of foolish mankind

## 개구리 교훈

개구리는
뛰어보고 말했다
이만큼 뛸 수 있다고
멍청해 보여도
자신을 알고 있다

사람은
말했다 뛰기도 전에
높이 뛸 수 있다고
뛰어보고 알았다
그게 아님을
인간의 자만심

## Baby’s Breath

How dare it lived so tenderhearted
how dare it lived with pure heart
the flower as it’s the baby’s breath
remain opened in white even dead
bowed head when the roses wilt
closed eyes when the human dies
the flower baby’s breath
you know the origin of life and death
shined the face of dead mothers
same as the baby’s breath
it’s more beautiful when it's together
even if we are separated
same as everlasting baby’s breath

## 안개꽃

얼마나 착하게 살았으면
얼마나 순결하게 살았으면
죽어서도 하얗게 피어있는
안개꽃
장미는 시들 때 고개를 꺾고
사람은 죽을 때 눈을 감는데
너는 생사본시를 알고 있으니
돌아가신 어머니들 저 모습으로
함께있어 아름다운 안개꽃처럼
우리 언제 헤어져도 안개꽃처럼

## Where is the Name

Searched a name in longing
may appear before I fell asleep
counted the names with fingers
only one may appear in dreams
no one name can just be found
going through so many names

## 찾을 수 없는 이름

잠들기 전에 보고 싶어 떠오르는
이름 하나 그리워 찾아보았다
꿈속에서라도 찾아올지 모르는
그 이름 하나 손꼽아 보았다
스치듯 지나가는 많은 이름들
금방 떠오르는 이름 하나 없었다.

## No Way

Lonely Grandpa alone in front of
the table in the kitchen corner
the wooden bowl on the table
just for him, made him look so sad
uncomfortable and trembling hands
spilt miso soup on the floor and
dropped his head to hide the tears
the grandchildren with their mom and dad
together at the main dining table
saw it, learned it, and remembered it
and asked to themselves
is that the way we do in the future.

## 이럴 수가

오직 그에게만 나무 밥그릇
놓인 식탁 앞에 홀로 앉은
할아버지 외롭고 불쌍해
불편한 맘 떨리는 손
눈물 섞인 된장국 쏟고 말았네
저 건너 가족과 함께 앉은 손자는
못 볼 것 보고 배워 기억하였다
내가 본 그 모습 내가 사는 이 세상
"나는 앞으로 어떻게" 하고 물었다

# Epilogue

*Poetry, a Reflection of Life*

## Remorseful Footprints

Every gap of layers of the time in life
when a moment of life open and folded
we call it the time and tide

Especially from the time when
the days I have lived is longer
than the time ahead of my life
the layers of time transformed into recollections

And about the time when
only I can look back the trace of my life
I just came to know
how many precious things I had forgot
and how many things I had lost in life

Despite of the things, fortunately enough,
as I had lived more with love and hope
rather than hatred and frustrations,
I could live tomorrow without any regrets

Some times in life
listening the layers of recollections play music
I wonder what makes my heart painful
and the tip of my nose chocked up
is that there is more repentance of the past life
rather than the missing things of the past

As the flowers bloom and fade
following the layers of seasons
so even among the layers of life
the enlightenment of repent and pity
self-reflection and happiness seem to bloom

I would like to live such a life
as I can hear the recollections play music
without any regret in the far future,
Always…….

## 돌아보면 아쉬움이

인생의 한순간이 열리고 접히는
그 시간의 갈피 사이사이를
사람들은 세월이라 부른다

특히 어느 때 살아갈 날보다
살아온 날들이 많아지면서부터
그 갈피들은 하나의 추억이 된다

자신만이 그 인생의 추억을
더듬어 볼 수 있을 무렵
얼마나 소중한 것들을 잊고 살았는지
얼마나 많은 것들을
잃어버리고 살았는지 알게 되었다

그나마 다행인 것은
미워하고 좌절하며 살아온 날들보다
사랑과 희망으로
살아온 날들이 많았기에
아쉬움은 있어도
후회 없이 살아갈 수 있었다

이따금 그 추억의 갈피들이
연주하는 노래를 들으면서
가슴이 아프고 코끝이 찡해지는 것은
단지 지나간 것에 대한 아쉬움보다
살아온 날들에 대한
미련이 많아서 일지도 모른다

계절의 갈피에서 꽃이 피고 지듯
인생의 갈피에서도
후회와 연민과 반성과 행복의
깨달음이 피어나는 것 같다

먼 훗날 추억이 연주하는 노래를
후회 없이 들을 수 있는
그런 인생을 살고 싶다.
늘…….

*Who Is This?*

## In Memory of My Love

Who is the one approached me in silence
placing a smile in the cup
as I enjoyed my morning tea

Who is the one approached me in soft steps
befriended with me and walking arm in arm
as I strolled along a path of fallen leaves

Who is the one came in the midst of rain
offering an umbrella
as I walked in a rainstorm

Who is the one drew a smile on the river
making me to miss the face even more
as I strolled along the windless riverbank

Who is the one made blooming from longing
in my youthful heart
as we wanted to live together among the flowers

Who is the one blew in with the wind
and built a nest in my heart
making me want to see forever

Who is the true one that stole my heart
making me want to see more and more
even though you are next to me

Oh, yes, my dear friend forever
you my dear love
you are the very one, the true one.

## 그대와 함께한 추억

차를 마시는데 소리 없이 다가와
찻잔에 담기는 그대는 누구입니까

낙엽 밟으며 길을 걷는데 살며시 다가와
팔짱 끼고 친구 되어주는 그대는 누구입니까

비를 맞고 걷는데 빗속으로 걸어 나와
우산을 씌워주는 그대는 누구입니까

바람 없는 강둑을 걷는데
물 위에 미소 짓는 얼굴 하나 그려놓고
더 그립게 하는 그대는 누구입니까

푸른 내 마음에 그리움을 꽃으로 피우고
꽃과 함께 살자는 그대는 누구입니까

내 마음의 주인이 되어
보고 있는데도 더 보고싶게 만드는
그대는 진정 누구입니까

아, 내 한평생 친구여

내 사랑하는 그대여

그대가 당신, 바로 당신이랍니다.

The attachment represent a summary of the author's life.

이 부록에 첨부된 기록은 작가의 삶을 정리한 이력서이다.

# Attachments / 부록

## 미국 국기 증서

THE ARCHITECT OF THE CAPITOL
1793

THE FLAG
OF THE
UNITED STATES
OF AMERICA

This is to certify that the accompanying flag was flown over the United States Capitol on August 2, 1988, at the request of the Honorable Tom Bevill, Member of Congress.

This flag was flown for Sung J. Lee, Ph.D.

George M. White
George M. White, FAIA
Architect of the Capitol

70682

The flag of The United States of America was flown for a day in 1988 at the Capitol Building in recognition of Dr. Sung jae lee's contributions as scientist and community services for the youth leadership development.

이 성조기는 이성재 박사의 과학자로서 미국의 과학기술 발전에 기여한 공로와 청소년 지도자 육성에 봉사한 공로를 치하하여 미국 연방의회 의원의 추천으로 국회의사당에 계양 되었음.

# 올해의 시집상

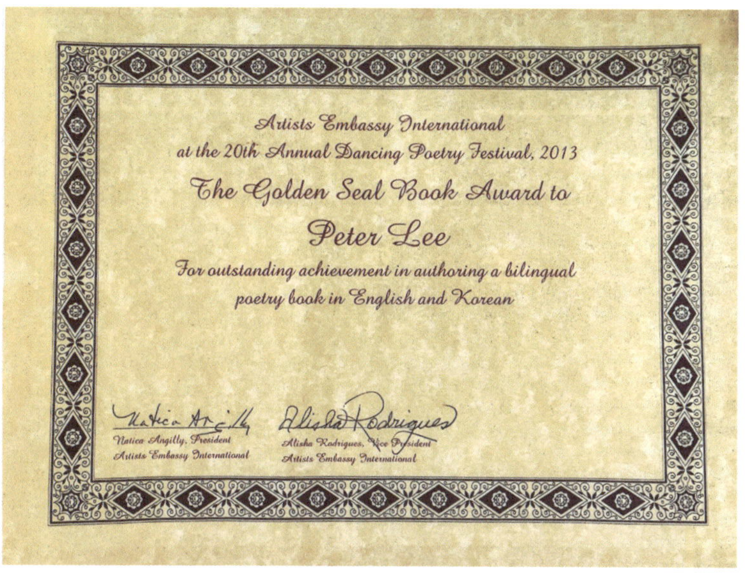

Artists Embassy International
at the 20th Annual Dancing Poetry Festival, 2013
The Golden Seal Book Award to
Peter Lee
For outstanding achievement in authoring a bilingual poetry book in English and Korean

Natica Angilly, President
Artists Embassy International

Alisha Rodrigues, Vice President
Artists Embassy International

Song of Poet, an anthology published in English and Korean received 2013 The Golden Seal Book Award

시인의 노애 (Song of Poet), 한영으로 출판된 시집은 샌프란시스코 명예의 전당에서 2013년 미국 문학 예술가 협회로부터 올해의 시집상 수상

## 효도대상 상패

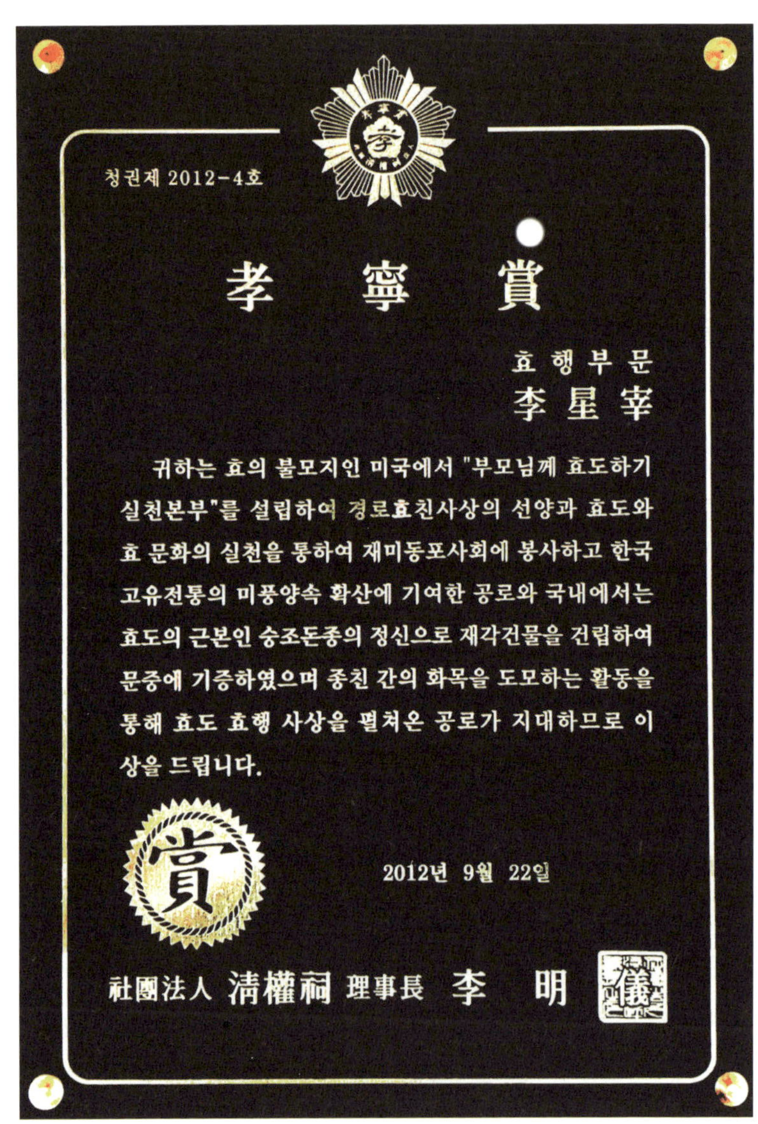
청권제 2012-4호
孝 寧 賞
효 행 부 문
李 星 宰
귀하는 효의 불모지인 미국에서 "부모님께 효도하기 실천본부"를 설립하여 경로효친사상의 선양과 효도와 효 문화의 실천을 통하여 재미동포사회에 봉사하고 한국 고유전통의 미풍양속 확산에 기여한 공로와 국내에서는 효도의 근본인 숭조돈종의 정신으로 재각건물을 건립하여 문중에 기증하였으며 종친 간의 화목을 도모하는 활동을 통해 효도 효행 사상을 펼쳐온 공로가 지대하므로 이 상을 드립니다.
賞
2012년 9월 22일
社團法人 淸權祠 理事長 李 明

Grand Award for filial devotion directed to Jeonju Lee Chosun Dynasty family and promoting filial teachings and activities in the Korean-American community in The United States

대한민국 청권사 조산왕조 전주이씨 대동종약원 효령대군파 종회로부터 2012년 효됴대상 수상

## 용덕재각 건물 사진

龍 德 齋

어머님과 함께 재각 앞에서

全州李氏大同宗約院孝寧大君波宗會洛州齋彦陽祖先塋下

崇 祖 惇 宗

Built and donated The Memorial Building "YongDeokJae" to Jeonju Lee Family Association, Kimhae District for ancestral worship in 1989

숭조돈종의 정신으로 토지와 성금을 헌성하여 1989년에 김해시 한림면 선영하에 용덕재(龍德齋) 재각 건물을 건립하여 전주 이씨 효령대군 낙주재 중시조 언양조 문중에 봉헌함